EMOTION WARS

EMOTION WARS

LOVE TO HATE

DAN world peace RECTOR

EMOTION WARS
LOVE TO HATE

iUniverse books may be ordered through booksellers or by contacting:

iUniverse
1663 Liberty Drive
Bloomington, IN 47403
www.iuniverse.com
1-800-Authors (1-800-288-4677)

Because of the dynamic nature of the Internet, any web addresses or links contained in this book may have changed since publication and may no longer be valid. The views expressed in this work are solely those of the author and do not necessarily reflect the views of the publisher, and the publisher hereby disclaims any responsibility for them.

Any people depicted in stock imagery provided by Getty Images are models, and such images are being used for illustrative purposes only. Certain stock imagery © Getty Images.

ISBN: 978-1-5320-8004-3 (sc)
ISBN: 978-1-5320-8006-7 (hc)
ISBN: 978-1-5320-8005-0 (e)

Print information available on the last page.

iUniverse rev. date: 08/09/2019

BE HONEST......

LOOK
WITHIN
YOURSELF

Dan Rector

LOVE AND SPECIAL THANKS TO

Andy

Bill

Carol

Pattie

Peter

Steve

CONTENTS

INTRODUCTION

CAUTION: This book will make you cry, laugh, hate and blame.

BUT

IF you are honest and your heart is open,

You will wake up
To find out
That YOU are
The eyes of the World!

MANKIND IS IN TROUBLE

Why talk about human beings?

Because human beings decide everything – from our relationships with "others" to why we are in misery or joy. We are all about our life, our children, our parents, our spouse, our enemies, our hopes, our dreams, our love. It's our world. It's everything.

But, there is a very, very serious problem with Human Beings. MANKIND IS IN TROUBLE.

It is not our IQ. Our IQ is very good. Our IQ took us to the moon and back, invented the web and discovered penicillin.

The problem is our Emotional Quotient (EQ). It's important to get things right and in order so "here" is the "COMBINATION" to understanding how our EQ is the culprit and why we are the last to know. This will be as simple as one, two, three, but first the biggest shocker is.......

Everything is made up! By that I mean **everything**! That is why we can hardly agree on anything….from cultures and laws all the way to spouses. I am not going to refer to GOD or Religion in this book and I'm NOT a detailed person. If we want to look at The Big Picture of Life, details will get in the way. Besides, as Einstein said: "I (we) can always look it up."

Yes, everything is made up and guess who made it up? We did - human beings! Everything was made up before the Greeks and Romans, during and after the Greek and Romans. Aristotle and Plato made up their stuff while the rest of the world made up their stuff. When generations, cultures and empires went away, the next human beings came along to make up new stuff: new good and bad, new how to talk, new how to behave and new how and when to kill.

When human beings agree, everything works for a while; then, eventually, we end up in disagreement, anger and hate.

Be open to the possibility that mankind is in serious trouble and his emotional (and thinking) reality is what brought us to this trouble and keeps us there.

Here is the one, two, three combination to save the Human Race.

NUMBER ONE:

We are animals.

We are not better, different, nor more advanced than all the other animals. We are still evolving! Just because we call ourselves Human Beings doesn't mean we are not animals. Darwin may have defined evolution and survival of the fittest, but modern science is discovering what runs our lives: DNA, hormones, chemicals, and the fact that 98% of thought is unconscious. We may know we hate someone but not realize we want to murder them. We may want to murder someone and not really know why. Science has discovered that the brain grows, connects and changes physically in different directions and in different areas. This can be done just by meditating on various subjects.

We don't always know who we are hating, why we are hating, when we are hating. We do, though, know for sure that THEY are wrong, THEY are BAD and WE are RIGHT and WE are GOOD. There is a saying: "The universe is laughing at you…and you are the last to know!"

Along came Freud revealing the animal in us in the form of our PSYCHE with repressed, displaced and unconscious emotions, including anger (to name just one). I say we are animals with evil and wrong in us, looking toward goodness, NOT good people continually surprised and astounded by the bad in ourselves.

The most important thing in the world to understand is: If we continue to think human beings are good, we will continue to abuse, belittle, bully, suffer anger, hate, murder and war. If we wake up and admit we are mostly ANIMAL and dangerous and evil, we can start with a new order of mankind.

NUMBER TWO:

The world runs on emotions.

Negative emotions are who we are. We are full of the animal in us that shows up in our emotions. These emotions may be repressed but they wait to explode and lash out. Jealousy, greed, deceit, fear, guilt, shame, anger, revenge can manifest in lying, passive aggressive behavior, rumor mongering, and every day maligning. These emotions will "get you" from someone else, or yourself. You might run from these emotions, try to move on, act as if you are putting the issue behind you, suffer or cry. You might blame your issues on gender or on other people, your life or your parents. The world runs on emotion, negative emotions.

NUMBER THREE:

Negative emotions turn into one thing.....HATE.

Hate is everywhere and recognizable when we blame the OTHER. There is enormous self-righteous hate around us and in us.

Hate doesn't stop when there is reasoning, logic, love, a spouse, children, forgiveness, or money. Hate will never stop. Hate is what human beings do best. Hate turns into alienation, murder, genocide, you name it.

Look, if you found dead bodies all the time and the only common denominator was a specific germ, wouldn't you want to identify that germ? YOU CAN! That germ in human beings is HATE!

Now that you are wearing different glasses, can you clearly see: It's not men against women? It's not the South against the North? It is not the Protestants against the Catholics? It's not Blacks against Whites? It's not children against their parents? It's not the color of skin or the rich against poor, educated against undereducated, generation X against Millenniums? It's not SUPERGIRL against SUPERMAN?

It's HATE!

Why do we hate? We have negative emotions. Where did we get negative emotions? We are animals. The arguably smartest man of the 20th Century said: "With the invention of the nuclear bomb, everything has changed, except the way man thinks." Albert Einstein.

Emotions are behind all thinking.

Stephen Hawkins said: "To survive, man will have to go to another planet."

They were referring to the hate human beings have and the extinction of our species.

Do you think these men are stupid?

Einstein made up the equation $E = MC^2$.

Dan Rector made up the equation ANE = H.

Animal + Negative Emotion = Hate.

Which of the equations has the potential to save mankind?

THE LAST WORD:

Until we become convinced that "it's" not out there but "it" is inside of man, meaning hate, we will continue to be the most dangerous animal on the planet.

For example, there is a difference between feeling anger towards someone, like we all do, and playing out those feelings with the intent to kill mentally, emotionally or physically. There is a difference between not wanting to work with someone and telling lies to get them fired, effecting their wife and children.

A true story:

Koko was a gorilla that understood 2,000 English words, in addition to using over 1,000 GSL signs. Her caregiver saw that Koko had pooped on the floor and signed:

"Koko bad. Koko pooped on floor."
Koko signed back: "No. I no poop on floor. YOU Poop on floor."

BEING JUDGEMENTAL

Judging others is what we do all day long, every day. It's a natural knee-jerk response in our mind and heart. Why do we judge others? We just do. When you judge someone, do you always throw in your BAD judgement of yourself? No! Do you judge everyone? No! You judge who you want, how you want, and NOT YOURSELF! What a scam, a game using only one way of seeing life.....your tainted view. Remember the double edged sword, if YOU judge someone it is like a drop of water you throw on them. If THEY judge YOU, it is like a hurricane visited upon you.

In my opinion, 99% or more of all judgements are wrong.

The human ego, the part of us that says I am superior and you are inferior, our self-righteousness, our gossip, I am bigger, better, faster than you, is a monster. While you talk… the ego is on the back burner, getting hot with judgmental rage, while you try to hold a pleasant face and a serene demeanor.

Judgmentalism is like a basket in your psyche. Everything someone says, everything someone does or doesn't do is judged and every single time the JUDGER doesn't agree or like something about YOU.....the judger writes on a little piece of paper with your name on it that says NO GOOD. Then, the psychological hate on that paper goes into your psychological basket. That basket can hold millions of little judgement papers. Sooner or later the owner of that basket cashes that basketful of judgements in for a PAY-OFF which could be murder, suicide or anything between. It will be cashed in all about how bad or wrong THE OTHERS are. The passive-aggressive "I'm ok, YOU are not ok, is like we are pretending to be Judge Judy.

So that's you, us. We judge others and that becomes our own karma. The human mind is sick, to judge others reflects who we really are, not THEM.

Are we being fair, honest and wanting good consciousness or are we resentful, maybe revengeful? I am better than you??

We are going to fill the basket, because we are full of negative emotions. The question is do we just dump out the baskets contents or dump those contents on top of other people? That is our decision.

THE LAST WORD

One thing is for sure, instead of having dignity, respect, humility, honesty and grace we choose to judge. We have different DNA, different parents, we are a different gender, we had different life experiences, and yet we continue to harshly judge, and put all our disgusting animal crap on others.

Remember, if a hundred people wrote down the definition of a cow, you would get a hundred completely different definitions. That is simple understanding. But if a hundred people judged a bum on the street, would they know that his children were killed in a car crash or he was once on the School Board?

Everyone thinks they see everything and know everything but don't realize the answer is inside of their own self.

When we judge another person, we always think we are right. We enjoy our self-righteousness but in fact we only have one chance to be right about anything and the universe (all other possibilities) has a zillion chances to be right! If we knew enough facts, enough feelings and enough information, we'd never be so condemning.

Do you know this story?

A man is traveling on a subway and his young grandchildren are jumping around on the seats and yelling. A passenger gets sick of it and yells at the man. The man says in a sad voice he is sorry. He was only trying to let the boys play and let off steam. "Their mother just passed at the hospital and we don't know what to do with ourselves."

Negative judging becomes Karma.

Let's try to be good to OURSELVES as well as OTHERS.

BEING ADVERSARIAL

Being adversarial is the biggest brick in the wall. That brick (prick!) is bigger than the Berlin wall and longer than the Great Wall of China. That brick becomes a psychological BARRIER to each other. Once judgmentalism turns into the brick of being adversarial, you are done!

Here's how the brick works. Every person is Judgmental. When we stop loving, caring, getting money, sex, a ride to work…our wonderful judgements become negative emotions. We are not judging now, we are blaming. Quickly the blaming turns to harder emotions such as dislike, anger, frustration and hate. The blame gets bigger and the reaction stronger. From passive-aggressive resentment comes the psychological ultimate: FIRING UP THE BIG BRICK!

We punish….by not talking to you, maligning you, gossiping about you, spreading rumors about you, and just plain hating you. Then of course, we murder you, physically, psychologically, legally and/or emotionally. AND we claim this action is all YOUR FAULT. Of course, some people are sincere and get an asterisk, a save. Instead of a brick they respond with an empathetic: "I am sorry for your pain." Why: Because they try to unite, to talk thru their problem, to say "I'm sorry," to forgive. How about this: they try to tell the truth, no matter how painful, to be cured in the moment.

It's funny, we can fight with one another, hate, go to war and kill, suffer disease and pain, murder, say horrible words to one another and pretend to be so strong. However, we can't do one thing in life because we are so weak. What is that? Look someone we love in their face and say we are sorry. It can be just as hard to receive those words. One thing we find hard as a decent human being is to **be** a decent Human Being.

If you are the family dog, or mom, or a good friend with a car, or a big brother with good advice, or a girlfriend that's attractive, or a boyfriend with "extra" money, you are a keeper! Nothing adversarial here until the dog gets old, mom becomes a bitch, the car breaks down, big brother sounds stupid, the hot and wealthy friend with benefits doesn't give enough. Then, we **decide** to be ADVERSARIAL.

Yes, all of these people become toast. Why? Because when we become adversarial we BECOME the toaster. You, Me, US, we are the toaster!

Being adversarial is mean, passive aggressive and will cause a person to lie, steal, and be stubborn beyond comprehension. It can wait 27 days or 27 years to say the word: checkmate. Hater! So sad, so sick, such a loss of joy and togetherness.

THE LAST WORD

If you find yourself pushing back against someone, STOP! They are going to hate you beyond belief. Why? Because once they stop being nice-nice, once they decide you are to blame, once they don't want to make it better, the animal in them has no reason not to be against you!

The wall is up.

You'll never get on the other side of the wall. You can knock on the cement door, send a letter of great sincerity, say I Love You, say I am sorry, say let's start over, say a million things but nothing will work. It won't work because we are animals….not good human beings, yet.

NARCASSISTIC

Here is the simple definition of a narcissist: Me! Me, me, me, me, me. NOT YOU!

Self-absorption, self-obsession displayed in all its ways, including absolute entitlement. Narcissism is not just vanity. When the ego can't get out of the box, it brings everything "into" the box. It's mine, it's mine, damn you….it's mine!

Someone will bake a delicious apple pie and give it to you. Someone will cut you a large slice of that apple pie and give that to you. Some person will take THEIR slice of pie and cut it in half, sharing with you. A mother, or another giving person, will insist on you taking THEIR piece of apple pie.

A narcissist will trick you or deceive you to steal your whole apple pie. Mine, NOT YOURS!!

Opportunity makes a thief but the narcissist is a thief 24/7.

All people are a little selfish. All people make mistakes. Most people have a conscious. Not the people that are narcissistic, psychopaths or have borderline personality disorders. These people have the same core, lack of empathy and lack of respect. To them, everything is about ME. LOOK AT ME, DAMN YOU LOOK AT ME! This is why they are different and why they cause harm to other human beings.

A Narcissist is like a black hole in outer space, nothing can get away from them and their entitlement. Everything is the narcissists: your attention, your dreams, your children, your family, your life, your everything!

For example, there is a difference between feeling anger towards someone, like we all do, and playing out those feelings with the intent to kill mentally, emotionally or physically. There is a difference between not wanting to work with someone and telling lies to get them fired, effecting their wife and children.

THE LAST WORD

You see, human beings are not just narcissistic, we are neurotic as hell.

We used to hold a mirror to our face, like Sleeping Beauty, and it was one-on-one. Now, unfortunately, the mirror is the world-wide web! People far away, poor people, people that were likely in harmony are watching daily the negative emotions and negative events over the world. There is goodness and hope and positivity...but it competes with culture war, emotional war, crime, hate, and of course actual truth vs fake truth.

This is going into everyone's thinking and psyche. Jealousy, anger, resentment, a variety of emotions are being viewed in that hand-held mirror.

Instead of realizing the person (human being) holding the mirror has the problem, we look into the mirror and say "mirror mirror the problem is THOSE OTHER PEOPLE."

The universe is laughing at us and we are the last to know it.

EMOTIONS

Emotions run the world.

Emotions run your life and everything you think. Your emotions are before your thoughts and after your thoughts. Emotions are the most powerful thing in the world. Thinking may have invented the atom bomb and dropped that bomb, but it was emotions that lead the thinking to the creation of the bomb. It was emotions that felt the results of the bomb having been dropped.

Emotions are about everything. They are unseen, unknown, yet as obvious as your facial reactions. They hate your best friend, love your best friend and the reason why you go to bed with your best friend's spouse.

Emotions control you far more than you control them. The greatest tennis players say it is not winning the match that drives them but it's the FEAR of losing. Yes, it is jealousy, fear, anger, hate, revenge, etc., that we fear we won't be able to stop, or even admit we feel. We prefer to think our emotions are always someone else's fault. Look at the Presidents of the U.S. and you will find emotions connected to sexual misconduct, enormous drinking and assassinations. You didn't know this? Then they cover up these emotions of greed, entitlement, inadequacy, and shame and they won't admit it.

We could tell each other stories of the power of emotion in our lives and how those emotions run the world.

One powerful story was told by Senator Edward Kennedy in his book **True Compass**. Teddy heard his father getting up one Sunday morning at their home in Cape Cod. John, his older brother, was sleeping on the sofa on the first floor. John hears his dad's footsteps and knows that he is supposed to be at Mass with his mother. John, fearing his Dad finding him there instead of at church, jumps up and scrambles out the window, running feverishly across their side yard. He jumps the fence and runs behind the neighbor's house…out of sight. At that time John F. Kennedy was the most powerful person in the world, President of the United States of America, and had won the Pulitzer Prize for his book: PROFILES IN COURAGE.

Emotions are who we are as Human Beings! Sure, we depress, oppress, suppress and repress our emotions automatically and unconsciously but they are in us, controlling us more than we can imagine. Emotions are what we hide, are afraid of, and sometimes release when we are in a rage, drunk or driving a car. Emotions never step down or go away. In fact, they are in our dreams at night, in our blood with hormones and in our breath. Our voice can barely hide our real emotions. We only think we are hiding them.

Emotions run our life from beginning to end. We think we are logical, good thinking planners and in control when in reality the FORCES of emotions are our primary life. As your mom, dad, dog, best friend…. everything we do to love them is about our emotions. Do you love your parents? Do you have kids? Did you get divorced? Do you work all the time and worry? Why? Emotions.

Emotions are like primary colors. You may see millions of colors, shades and combinations. These come from the primary colors. Your favorite color may be red, you may have anger issues. Your favorite color is blue, you may be a calm person.

Science is discovering such things as prisoners coming before the Parole Board have a better chance of a favorable outcome if the parole panel has just had breakfast or lunch, changing their mood and emotions.

If we ever understand the chemicals in the human brain fully enough, we would see clearly what is running us, what runs the world, why mankind doesn't get along and why eventually we will (unless we realize what I just said) blow up the planet.

We are getting angry and emotional at the wrong people. We need to get angry at ourselves for not holding on and doing something about the consciousness of our negative emotions.

Emotions are like a buoy you have in a body of water. You think the buoy is far from you and you think it's BELOW the water, but it is attached to your legs. The buoy will always have the first words of your life and the last. You think you are a good swimmer and you are in control, but the moon and the tide know what is going to happen.

THE LAST WORD

Carl Jung said nothing effects thinking like feelings and nothing effects feelings like thinking. I say feelings (emotions) effect thinking first and foremost. Remember, 98% of thought is unconscious and we don't know our own evil intents! We do know, however, our bad, negative and disastrous results: fighting, failed relationships, divorce, negative response to love, lack of forgiveness, misunderstandings, and so forth.

Yes, emotions are a war, a weapon, a sad condition that runs the world. They may have ruined your childhood, your marriage or a nuclear arms meeting. Knowing this we won't put the study of emotions first on this planet, we will just look at the air, the water, the nuclear build up (emotionally) and continue to do our favorite emotion – HATE.

THE EGO

The Ego is a monster, the biggest monster that can possibly be. It's bigger than the universe. It's deceptive and dominating but dominating who?

The Ego can be thought of as an alligator. The alligator looks still, perhaps very slow. The mouth opens and you are intimidated by the size of that mouth and those teeth. He's not close to you so you feel safe. So safe that you decide to walk by it. Suddenly it speeds up, runs you down and eats you!

You could decide to walk behind the alligator and the powerful tail knocks into you, breaking your leg and you get eaten. You could see the gator basking in the sun and laying on the sand so still, he looks like he is not going to move for hours. You decide to go for a swim. He silently sneaks into the water, grabs you and locks on pulling you deep down. You are buried in the vines that grow near the bank where he comes back later to enjoy his meal!

The Ego is always hungry, always right, always better than others. Sometimes it's in your face, sometimes it's violent, sometimes it's quiet. Being passive aggressive, sometimes The Ego waits for years till it GETS YOU.

The Ego will never give up, never give in and will never admit anything if caught red handed. It will kill you, sometimes pushing you to commit suicide before admitting anything.

Ego is the heart of deception, the hand of self-righteousness, and the ultimate liar in life!

Ego can be bigger, faster, stronger or better....or a snake in the grass. You won't know the Ego until you become conscious of a person's actions, then it's too late. For a good con man, the Ego is an easy playground of deceit, manipulation and stealing. Whether it be your Ego or the Ego of your best friend, spouse or sibling, we all live on that playground.

Why is the Ego so powerful, deceiving, negative, MURDEOUS?

Because the animal in us is much more animal than good. Also, the Ego in our animal self has not evolved enough or been honest yet. What GOT US HERE....hate, murder, look at me, I am more good than bad, KEEPS US HERE. I want what I want when I want it our Ego screams.

THE LAST WORD

When we realize all of this we can be born again. We can put love, kindness, honesty and integrity first, leaving our animal self.

In Casablanca, Humphrey Bogart puts the love of his life on an airplane with her husband, sending them away. Why? His ego was honest and fearless. He speaks his "new" words: "Here's looking at you, kid."

POLITICAL CORRECTNESS

Being politically correct (PC) is something made-up to get "respect." It gets control of people, or tries, brain-washing them into believing they are supposed to like not just SOME but ALL people. After all, if church doesn't work, or rules, or the law, then make up the LOVE OF POLITICAL CORRECTNESS. If you aren't PC, you'll be called a racist, someone who is against equality and perhaps a selfish person.

Let's get something straight, political correctness is good. It's needed. It's fair. Especially for the good people who do good. PC is a bad thing when it is inappropriately installed or enforced. The worst bad in the world is BAD people thinking they are doing GOOD against alleged BAD people!

When we try to make everyone do right and good and equal, what are we really doing?

Political Correctness is made-up and pushed on people and society; without respect we act our bad normal and our bad natural ways. By that I mean we all have our opinions, prejudices, likes and dislikes. We all don't like something in other people. So, to not like everyone is normal. What are you going to do about it?

If you have respect, you don't have to be fake with your likes and dislikes with people or with life. The key is respect. Why do you think Asia has been bowing for thousands of years? When you have respect, you can have empathy, understanding and kindness.

Political correctness puts all people in one box and tells us how to act and think. Why? Because it's the government, The Left, The Right or the OTHER telling us how to respect. It is as if laughing spontaneously, or at the wrong time, or too loud, and having tears falling down from our eyes is the wrong way to laugh. The government is going to tell you and others when and how to laugh, and react, but don't be too loud!?

Life is full of natural diversity without our self-righteousness. An example: Let's say two dozen people go to 31 Flavors for an ice cream. There are 31 flavors. Who orders first? How many scoops: one, two or three? What type of cone is chosen? What flavors of ice cream and in what order? Pay with cash, credit or debit card? Borrow money from your friend with you? Sit inside or out? The odds of any two people having or wanting the exact same thing is off the chart. People can be together with many differences and outcomes.

Such a life.

I'm overweight and if an overweight person sits next to me I might not like it. If they smell a little, I might not like that either. If they annoy me, I might move. Have I had this reaction to someone else in my life? Of course! So what?

Life is full of our opinions, rejections, likes and dislikes. To tell us being normal is that we like everyone is simply not true. We pick our friends, mates, the good guy in the movies, books we like and we have to be careful of Big Brother's Stuff.

Political correctness is needed sometimes. For the human being, it is all about one beautiful, glorious human word....RESPECT.

THE LAST WORD:

When I see children, I think they are beautiful and precious, whatever skin color or background. When I see old people unable to do well, I feel empathy and compassion whether they were a garbage collector or a lawyer. When I see dogs I like them joyfully, no matter if they are purebreds, half breeds, bastards or bitches! If I see a pit bull growling at me, I walk away. I don't care about political correctness, I care about respect!

RACISM

There is no such thing as Racism, it is a manifestation. Racism is the result of hate – not the hate itself!

Sure, on one hand we blame, we hate, we perpetuate the color card all around the world. We argue the fact, the situation. Who is better? Who's more right?

I have a black friend and asked him "what about all the good white folks that fought for your freedom and died?" He said: "I hate them, too."

I truly apologize for the original slavery and cruelty and murder in the U.S. However, what about slavery, cruelty and murder around the world and through all history? The answer is: we are all human beings and only 4% genetics separates us from chimps, making us genetically closer than the mouse is to a rat. Why argue about race when it is just a reflection of hate down deep?

If all human beings were the exact same color and 5' 10" tall with a million dollars, we would hate the people with the million dollars in their front pocket.....not the ones with the million dollars in their back pocket! The CORE hate that I am talking about is who we all are, not the manifestation of fragmented racial arguments.

Be a Doctor of Human Beings. Blood may be the same color in all human beings but that color is Hate. Forget skin color.

Richard Pryor said: "Forget about racism. It's bad enough being a person." Genius. He is saying the same thing I am saying without the word Hate. You know hate, it is stronger than love, or else we wouldn't have thousands of nuclear bombs.

Human beings don't like other human beings, they blame each other. They blame and hate the other group. Human Beings don't like their mother or their father, their brothers, sisters, coworkers, bosses, other cultures, other counties, other drivers, neighbors, people that own guns, people that don't own guns. People have one thing in common. HATE.

Is there any difference in hating those we choose to hate: a bald man, a fat woman, a young person with too many tattoos, a person talking too loud, a person with too much money, bad drivers? We simply choose who and what we want to hate. People are mean and cruel to children, spouses, workers, old people, handicapped people and only the N word is banned??

The color is on our skin. The hate is in our heart.

THE LAST WORD

Everything is made up. The hate is right. The hate is justified. The hate is the important hate. I won't hate that group, I will hate this group. It's not about ME. It is not about MY character. It's not about MY integrity.

I know who to hate.
I know how to hate.
I am right in my hate.
Life is an inside job.

Only a blind man does not see color.
Only a transfusion of consciousness will change HATE.......to LOVE.

FREEDOM OF SPEECH
(YOU CAN'T SAY!)

You can't say ANYTHING that won't offend someone. That's insanity. The First Amendment, the very first amendment, is Freedom of Speech.

Why would a society believe Freedom of Speech is a right given to its people, when you can't say anything that will offend someone?

Being politically correct and blaming individuals that express an opinion or say something by which all people are not offended is in itself implied guilt of the speaker. Now, instead of having one person (the listener) stymied or with perceived offense, you have millions not able to talk. Does it change their personality, change their heart, their soul? Of course it does! Not to mention affecting their personal joy, spontaneity, humor, positive teasing and most of all their freedom!

Is it better to never make a mistake, never say you are sorry, never learn from life or learn how to temper yourself in order to respect others? Is it better to have Big Brother do it for you? If so, all we are left with is fear.

The use of guilt, shame and fear is the best symbolic hanging a government can do. Can you imagine no Freedom of Speech, but Fear of Speech?

At an actual hanging, the only one that sees the truth is the man or woman looking thru the noose. He sees the shockingly large crowd. The smiles, the nervousness, the grins, the hate in the eyes of old friends, the close friends, the neighbors and family. There's no trial, there is now only a body hanging from the tree, while the crowd walks away with the shame and guilt that used to be blame.

The people that created this country, fought and died during the Revolutionary War and wrote the Constitution are sick to their stomachs now.

I know who put this on these United State of America and why.

Changing the subject a little, it is interesting that after we have made-up that we can't offend anyone, ever, that we can have some people say the "N" word and it is ok. No problem! What's wrong with saying that we ALL will have respect? Some people are OK to say the "N" word, in movies, songs, television shows, standing next to the black President of the United States at a celebrity roast. Should women use the "C" word, yet men can be fired for using it? Maybe we ALL should not say the "N" word or the "C" word. Maybe we should ALL be equal.

We made up the Politically Correct rules because we didn't want to offend particular groups of people. What if we became one group of people, human beings, and we were equal?

Right now, what got us here, keeps us here. It's okay to say the "N" word in front of television cameras and the world. However, if someone a few tables away in a coffee shop eavesdrops and hears you refer to the "N" word in a rap lyric, all they have to say is they are offended and call you a hater. Next thing you know, you are in front of that television camera. Actually, they are hating on you!

America has come to this? How stupid are human beings? How can we get something like Freedom of Speech so ass-backwards?

Our parents and their parents died in World Wars for our dignity and freedom and now we have to put duct tape over our mouths. For what? Most people, most of the time, are fine. Saying I'm sorry, leaving, lowering their voices or telling someone to mind their own business was normal and okay. What is not okay is our freedom to make mistakes is being taken away from us.

Don Rickles is choking on his matzah balls with a hockey puck in his ear!

Seriously, brainwashing is easy if you are willing to go "F..k" yourself. That is sad.

THE LAST WORD

Like I said, you can make a movie to make money about anything, using any kind of speech. Women can appear on television with their shirts completely open, forget that children could be watching. But, if you say something that MIGHT offend someone, it is life altering AND the criteria changes every day! You can accuse anyone of anything. Democrats and Republicans can hate each other and get nothing done while spouting outrageous accusations, offending the world! Our government can threaten nuclear holocaust. The government can threaten to shut the government down in a snit, and did!

We can buy all kinds of expensive guns, bullets and weapons of mass destruction, but we can't speak in a manner someone might find offensive. Really?

Who said this? For what reason?

I know, but I can't say. I would offend someone.

MEN

Men think with their other head. It's called a penis. Men are violent, it's a testosterone thing.

I can understand the frustration and anger women have with men: men are insensitive, forceful and domineering. Maybe men have the cart before the horse.

There are some good areas in men and it might show up in dads, teachers, hard working men, to name just a few. Even good men have one major problem: emotions/feelings. Most have trouble with intimacy, kindness, compassion, anger, outrage, empathy and condemnation of another person. Some other trouble men might have is the inability to talk, touch or be silent with another person.

A friend told me: "Most men aren't very good with feelings and emotions." A perfect example of this would be playing basketball without the basket. It's funny, if you mismanage money and not save, not only are you broke but people put blame on you as well. If you are stupid in life and do stupid things, people judge you and you are an outcast. If you are a man and not taking responsibility for effecting everyone around you emotionally and you are in denial and dismissing your emotions, then it's "well, men aren't good at feelings and emotions."

Emotional responsibility is a bitch. Men like to blame or take the easy way out: using anger, yelling, silence, violence. It's in their hormones, DNA, emotions. They are more animal than they will admit.

When people are dying, they often say: "Tell so-and-so I love them." Why not tell them now?

Men take the easy way out because it feels uncomfortable not to. The men of the WW II generation were not perfect, but their values included shaking your hand, looking you in the eye, speaking up, doing unto others as they would want done unto them. It's hard to do the minimum feelings with the web, fatherless homes, and men being cowards to speak up and lead by example. It is especially hard when not doing the appropriate emotions in life.

Men are pussys. It takes more John Wayne guts to tell the truth, to be sincere, to keep your word, to be on time, to laugh till you cry. It takes less guts to walk around pissed off, aggressive or silent in anger.

The Federal Violence Against Women (FVAW) Act was a long time coming. When I watch the television show COPS, I see a lot of men going to jail for domestic violence, as well as some women. This is a good thing! Violence has to stop. In one situation the man was handcuffed and being put in the police car when his wife yelled: "Yeah!! I f...ed your brother, and he was better than you." Which violent act came first, the physical or the emotional?

THE LAST WORD

Men will continue to be a weak, left handed person, ignorant, blaming and in despair until he sees that emotions run the world. He doesn't see the patterns in his life of failed love for parents, significant others, children, co-workers and life itself.

Men will not see the patterns of fear, anger, self-righteousness and false domination. Man's chant of "I am bigger, faster, stronger than anyone and everyone" still exists and dominates. They only feel the emotions going to HATE, which result in loss, war and death. Men have created the last minute to midnight on the Doomsday Clock.

John Wayne may be dead and buried somewhere in the hard ground but he is shaking in his boots. Why? Because after being the most awesome REAL MAN in people's minds, he finally knows that his best self was the gentle, kind, strong, good giant that he could have become.

WOMEN

Women want it all. They have a vagina. They are passive-aggressively violent.

Freud said women don't know what they want. He was wrong. They want children and they don't take responsibility for that desire. It's okay to want children, but when you don't wait, don't plan, don't save, don't put your life in order, don't pick decent boys and don't use protection women have children. When you do get a good trainable decent man instead of one of the bad boys, you have a shot at a good family life.

Yes, women want that baby. Their first dream is about their wedding day, their finest moment, the dress, the flowers. The dream is about what comes next, the house with the white picket fence. First what is needed is the MAN.

Men don't have this dream, they are the followers. Years later, women go through more men, more blame from drama, divorce and unfulfilled, unrealistic expectations. Did Cher really expect Greg Allman to cut the grass on Sunday morning? They still have their children in their life, but the damage is done. Negative emotions from women are responsible.

As I said before, men don't do feelings and emotions and women have different and more buttons for their emotions. Men are naturally with their hormones and muscle violence. Women have their period, the moon, and their own hormones and abundant negative emotions.

Women have emotions that are wonderful, too. They can be exceptionally kind, giving, nurturing, intelligent, intuitive, romantic, adventurous, mystical and mysterious. The problem is they want a lot with those emotions (love, family, success at work) but if they are too egotistical, self-righteous, revengeful, manipulative, or spiteful it leads to destruction.

Yes, having a vagina is like having a big house that accumulates many things, both good and bad. Accumulations such as beauty, children, self-righteousness, ego, anger, helping, condemnation and excitement!

Men may be fighting Dad by going off to war with their guns and missals to kill all the humans they can. Women stop fighting Mom and own a man of her own. Men go around the world killing men but women kill men one at a time, dragging them into her house. Men are the weaker sex and women know it, making men clueless!

The responsibility is on the women. And what do they do? They blame men and take their children, instead of women cleaning up their own house. The female psyche of being bigger, better, faster than men is on the other shoe now, women's shoes. Women play out their negative emotions on men, the biggest dummy.

The emotions of women have turned to HATE and have not won anything instead of uniting with children and a man, as first wanted before the wedding. Unlike men that go off to work to win but fail because they don't have honest feelings; women may go to work but end up alone and revengeful, empty.

THE LAST WORD

Women will continue to be overly emotional people that manipulate while being passive-aggressive, the right-arm of mankind, not taking responsibility that **emotions run the world.**

Women don't see the pattern in their lives of failed love for parents, boyfriends, spouses, children, friends and life itself. They will not see their insatiable wants and ego! Their negative emotions rage fully and go to HATE, which results in loss and emptiness.

Watching Oprah for a quarter of a century didn't make women stronger, wiser, or more beautiful. Nor did it help create a united family. Watching made women even more fragmented.

If Oprah was right about weight, her lifelong dream boyfriend and her EGO the size of a Great Gatsby mansion, why doesn't it show?

Human beings constantly put the cart before the horse. In Oprah's case, the cart was "full" of stuff and the horse was named, False God.

Dishonesty, denial, and adversarial blame is everywhere.

MEN AND WOMEN

Men and women are two completely different creatures.

When women's brains are scientifically tested for electrical activity, it shows a lot of activity over both hemispheres evenly distributed, Women use everything up there, including enormous amounts of "juice" from their hormones.

Men, on the other hand, have much less activity in both hemispheres. But wait….where they do have activity there is much more of a concentration **and** that light is very dense No pun intended! They are the "Hunter." LOL

Do you know that women use about 23,000 words a day compared to men's 7,000 words a day? Emotions? I think so.

If two couples are going to a restaurant, they are in very different worlds. The men are looking forward to a steak, baked potato, chips and salsa, a beer. Make that a big steak with two beers! The women discuss the cost and have figured out everything about the restaurant before going. At the restaurant the women are all about the ambiance, the bathroom, their look. There will be a lot of gossip at that table and a lot of intense psychological study…that the men are clueless about. The menu will be studied and studied and much later she'll eat. After one glass of wine, maybe more!

Men and women are almost equal at being egomaniacs and self-righteous. They just do it differently. These forces are all played out in negative emotions — like two tornados.

Men and women meet, fall in love, everything perfect at the start. Then, judgmentalism, blame and anger come in from both sides. Remember, judgmentalism is written down on little sheets of paper and put in each of their "Baskets" in the psyche. Millions of little sheets are written, without understanding or forgiveness, or change of character. These sheets of paper build up and all of a sudden – POW. Divorce.

Millions and millions of people get divorced and they are convinced it's all about their story and they blame the other. Every single member of a divorcing couple will blame the other person creating the germ of HATE, which will always be there. Hate will never be blamed. It was the other person....always the other person.

When a million times a million people's lives have been ruined, they never see Darth Vader, their own hate. Check the basket. It is full of self-righteousness and hate. We can either choose to believe that each person is right about the other person or we are haters. Think about it, every person originally thought the other was the greatest person in the world. Then, poof, away with the greatest and in with the worst. Did everyone make the same mistake? Did every divorcing person escape from the worst person in the world? How about it was the germ of **hate** in us. Are we going to be able to admit this?

So please pick one:

a} All of the divorced others are wrong

OR

b} The blame is **full of hate.**

Men and women are absolutely sure the other is the bad guy. Absolutely positive.

Let's look at some of this blame and hate.

Men yell, scream, break things and do violence to the physically weaker sex. They still don't get it. Women, for half a century have been so proud of their "toilet seat" condemnation of men. The toilet seat became symbolic of all men, their penis and their disrespect for women by leaving the toilet seat up.

The toilet seat was made to go perfectly up or down. It's used that way. Men always look to see if it's up or down. Women who live alone or with other women don't have to look, but they always look in public places, for several reasons. Different people, different habits. Now if there are children in the home, that's different. Or if the woman asked the man to please leave the seat down. The opportunity could arise for both people to choose to "agree to agree."

Back to men. When in their self-righteousness, strength, acting adversarial, being stubborn, and not communicating well, men constantly show their inability to do feelings and emotions. What women forget is that men are like this toward men, driving some men crazy, too! Men have to wake-up. There are many children already grown up still waiting for their dad's approval, warmth and an "I love you." That's disgusting.

Almost every woman has a medium to large electrical device, possibly costing as much as $125.00 in her nightstand. This may have multiple speeds, turn mechanically in different directions and may be connected to an anal probe or a clitoris stimulator. All very high tech and color specific: black, red, tan, white, yellow. The vibrator is always ready for substitute action. Women love these machines and give them as presents, surprises or "share" it. Some women give it to their 15 year old daughters with instructions. Surprise! I love you. Vibrators come small. They fit in purses, in the coat pocket, in the panties. Another person can have control of the vibrator from their phone quite a distance away.

There is illegal porn that is, and should be, banned and is just bad and wrong. But men in general grew up looking at the pages of PLAYBOY and watching porn movies. Society says that's wrong, disgusting and men have to stop and be reformed. Would it be okay, better, if men's night stands had a mechanical self-lubricating vagina, with different speeds AND they could be used in public places discretely?

THE LAST WORD

That's what human beings do: "You are bad, not me."

What if the world wasn't Koko saying "You pooped, not me," but Koko and a male ape called King Kong?

Wait a minute.....

It IS!!!

CHILDREN

If music is the international language of the world, children are the notes to mankind. We know we have a heart when we have a child because our heart walks the earth. We have to love them. We have to protect them. They look up to us with their big eyes sparkling with life itself. Their hair shining, begging to be touched; their cheeks want to be patted. They want to be held in our arms for warmth and security. We share our heart beat and absolute unconditional love.

We love our children.

The positive emotions, the character, the integrity of being a good parent is paramount to society. Children are our life. In fact, we can divide our lives into before our children and after our children were born. A baby changes everything.

If something goes wrong, we will never leave our children. Bad things and disaster can happen: accidents, drugs, disease, decay. Immorality, evil and hate are everywhere. All or any of these may come.

Still, a good father, a good mother, will always love their children against people of revenge, cheating, lying and stealing.

Hate is everywhere.

How do you keep children away from hate? You can't. The hate germ is everywhere and will get on them and cause them to be sick, too. You hope, pray and try as hard as you can but hate is everywhere with every person. It moves from person to person just like a cough, cold or fever.

The ego doesn't want to hear "I'm sorry.' "Can we talk?" "Will you forgive me?" "I love you." "Will you give me another chance?" "Did you know this?" "Did you know that?" No one knows you and loves you like your parent. If you are a parent, you will know your parents are just like you: crazy in love with their child!

We would do anything for the good of our children. We would tell them the truth when they need to hear it, give them a gift we saved many years for, be silent for them, walk with them, change their child's diaper, as we did for them, tell them they are beautiful, that we love them just as they are. We will ask them to tell us how we hurt them. We will forgive them and ask them to forgive us. If we have been estranged and reconnect we will ask: "What's your favorite television show?" "What's your favorite movie?" "Are you happy?" "How can I be there for you?" "Can we have coffee together?" "Can we laugh together?" "Can we be honest?" "Can we talk, talk, talk?" "Can we hug hello?" "Can we hug goodbye?" This is what a parent does, or did, or wants.

When the germ gets on our children to be HURT and then BLAME, they won't want to go back to the PERSON they believe wronged them. It's understandable. The easiest way of dealing with tragedy is to never go back. But goodness, courage, honesty, integrity and love will always go back to see the original heart, the original goodness and make sure to give love one final chance. One final opportunity to be alive, good, free, happy and feel that you did the right thing and that you gave love, all the love you have. You go back and find out. You go and do what love taught you, not hurt but love.

A long time ago I came around the side of my house and found a bird on the ground trying to fly away. It was obviously not going to make it. I was wearing heavy boots and raised one above the bird's head. Before I stepped down to do away with the bird, I had a thought: "I can't kill it." I had never been in this situation before. I brought the bird into the house, put it in a box with grass and fed it bugs, all the time thinking this wouldn't work.

A week later I gave it another chance. I took it outside, looked at the sun and said: "Here goes." I raised my arms and "it" flew away! At that moment I was surprised and it became one of the happiest moments of my life. I still think about that day.

Another true story. An elephant in India was with her calf. A train came along and hit the calf, killing it. The next day the mother elephant returned to the exact same spot. The train came again, the elephant hit the train so hard it derailed.

THE LAST WORD

All you need is love
All you need is love
All you need is love, love
Love is all you need.

THE ENDING

If you have read this book this far, you are appropriately offended, pissed, and you have done what we all do, been judgmental, blamed someone, got angry, and possibly became enlightened to the fact that we humans are in serious trouble. We are. Remember: ANE = H. We humans are an animal with negative emotions that turn to hate. Do you see hate in the world? Do you see hate in your family? Do you see the hate in yourself? Did you see hate in your divorce? Do you see jealousy or passive aggression at work? Does everyone hate someone at work?

Hate is not about the facts, the story, the other, the group over there, the other country or even the other ideology. Hate is not the skin color or the way someone looks. Hate is in our blood. If we were all 5' 10" millionaires and had the same religion, we would hate each other even more because some people would be right handed, others would be left handed. The worst sons of bitches would be those people that were ambidextrous! We would hate the ugly people, too!

The germ that leads to adversarial behavior, blaming, killing and murdering is hate!

There are hundreds of tv shows and movies about crime and murder. Possibly 1,000 shows since the invention of television. We incessantly watch these on extra-large screens showing amazingly clear color the stories of crime, hate, suicide, sexual abuse, mystery and murder.

Why?

Because of the law of attraction.

Around the world we cut fingers off, rape, stone, decapitate, experience genocide and threaten the world with nuclear total destruction.

Why?

Negative emotions and hate.

We will continue to blame every possible thing in our world on someone other than ourselves and we will not take responsibility for our being an animal. An animal with negative emotions that can't, or won't, admit our reality is hate.

Hate is first on the crime scene, last to leave the crime scene and sometimes is covering up the crime scene.

Why?

Because we continue to use and **BE** hate. What got us here as haters, keeps us here. Yeah, don't blame hate; that finger would only point back at us instead of those people.

That damn hate is judgmentalism, turned into self-righteousness, with resentments then stored in the basket in our psyche. Passive aggressive anger, overt anger, jealousy, fear, manipulative behavior, lying, cheating, stealing, and blame all simmer until they become hate—naming just a few possible negative feelings and emotions. Yes, this is who man was, is, and will be until we admit who we really are…..not who we say we are.

At home, at work, in the media, in the government, in the world, we are blamers that hate. We are also murderers. You think our negative emotions are only emotions? Look to the prisons. Look at the world. Do you think murder only happens physically?

The emotions leading to murder may come slowly and never be delivered physically, but yet will be in everyone's life, every day. It doesn't have to be physical to be murder. Our deep thoughts and feelings of being glad or ever so slightly happy that someone got fired, or lost their dog, has been diagnosed with cancer, got divorced, lost a loved one, the list can go on endlessly. Remember Bob Dylan's song POSITIVELY FOURTH STREET: "You've got a lot of nerve to say you are my friend when I was down you just stood there grinnin'."

Yes, we are always hating and murdering others, if not physically, emotionally or passive aggressively, then covering up the crime scene. Thus we gossip, malign, and have negative emotions towards others. But, we love our dog enormously, animal to animal.

One last thing on humans, the hater, the murderer. When we can't get that hate out onto others, we carry it on our shoulder and in our heart. That's why we are so unhappy. We become alone with our hate and then perhaps depressed (Freud said: Depression is anger turned inward), sad, angrier at ourselves and perhaps suicidal. This hate and murder must get out or it goes inward. Call it energy... powerful negative energy.

Like a pathological liar, kleptomaniac, self-defeating person or bullying person, who is going to admit this? The only way to claim it, is to name it.

This book is not about a false end of the world. The end of the world is not going to be a Nostradamus event, an alien thing, probably not a meteor (what are the odds?). It's not going to be warming of the earth, yet. The END could be in your beliefs and faith, (I am not doing religion). One thing is for sure: man's history of war, negative emotions and hate can and will exterminate the animal called man from the face of the earth. The stage is set and has been for 70 years.

Yes, the last 70 years have been an illusion. We feel since WW III hasn't happened, it might not happen. Wrong! Since the Cuban Missile crisis there have been several close nuclear exchanges between Russia and the U.S. Aides to presidents have told all. In the 1980's Russia was informed that we, and other countries, were going to have a nuclear drill... just a test. We had taken part in drills many times before. What could go wrong? Well, for some reason, Russia believed we were going to pre-empt a first strike to catch them off guard. Russia almost beat us to the extinction game!

China has a lot of nuclear missiles, not talked about, in the belly of her mountains. Do you know China has grown in every way and can only keep spreading their navy, currency, wealth and culture around the world like the US did? Do you know America is already at war economically, territorially (in the oceans, outer space, information, high tech, satellites), and espionage, etc., with ALL countries in tension around the world?

Have you read Ted Koppel's book, LIGHTS OUT? This is about the loss of our electrical grids and the power we use to live on. Did you read Garry Kasparov's, the best chess player ever, book WINTER IS COMING? He knows Putin and Russia well. He also knows that every large city in China and Russia has nuclear missiles aimed at them from the United States to eliminate them. Likewise, every city in the United States could be blown up.

Here is the biggest factor. When all of these missals blow up the earth, dirt will fill the sky and radiation particles will stay in the atmosphere, covering the Northern Hemisphere. Then, the particles will work down to the Southern Hemisphere, blocking the sun and killing all life, plants and animals, creating Black Winter.

Putin has already publically said during a nuclear event he will go into the mountains for 5-8 years before coming out and that we would never find him.

Do you know that certain governments have made underground tunnels to escape the world on top and are prepared right now? Do you know that some counties have nuclear tunnel diggers that can dig 20-30 miles a month? Do you know that our Washington government can go underground from DC to the Ozark Mountains? Do you know that their hideaways have plants, animals, an air supply, military, hotels, and a totally prepared way of life already planned?

THE LAST WORD

Remember when the night was lit up with bombs landing on Bagdad, Iraq, sent there by President George W. Bush? The world was changing.

The next day north of Chicago on a busy street, in a tiny suburb, a grey haired lady was standing alone on a busy corner holding a sign: NO WAR. Hours later, she was still there holding her sign with just those two words. Was she a blaming, hating, murdering, egomaniac?

Do you know John Lennon's song IMAGINE?

Imagine there's no countries
It isn't hard to do
Nothing to kill or die for
And no religion, too
Imagine we the people
Living life in peace.

Was he some pot head, blathering about WW III?
(Imagine was voted the song of the century.)

Remember this:
Albert Einstein said: "With the invention of the nuclear bomb everything has changed, except the way that man thinks."

Steven Hawking said: "To survive, man will have to go to another planet."

Koko said: "I didn't poop there, you pooped there."

Dan Rector says:

"People of the earth, WAKE THE FUCK UP!!!"

THE PROBLEM

The problem is not 15,000 nuclear bombs and missiles, which are just a manifestation. The problem isn't over THERE. The problem isn't THOSE people....that group... that country....the color of THEIR skin. **The problem is US....ALL OF US!** We have the only destructive germ on earth. The only germ able to wipe out 7 billion people – AT ONCE!!!

THE BIG BANG didn't happen a long time ago, it's going to happen soon. It's called WW III.

THE ANSWER

What got us here, keeps us here: blaming, hating, murdering, genocide, world wars. Something is terribly wrong with us. What is it? It's our negative emotions and we are in denial that we have them. Where are our negative emotions? In our brains. They are physical maps in our heads drawn by hormones, chemistry and negative electrical activity. Science has clearly revealed this and is still discovering proof of what runs our lives — NEGATIVE EMOTIONS. We say we are good and in control but we are disgustingly bad and out of control. We are in denial and adversarial and we take no responsibility for our hate. Everyone in the world is wrong – except **us**, so says the human brain and its chemistry.

If we put this thought FIRST in the world and say THIS is what is going to start WW III, **this** represents the GERM of mankind (hate). It is **our** responsibility to change, the right answer to the most horrific problem in the universe. By stopping our hatred of each other (which is our disgusting, weak, cowardly way of blaming the world and turning our negative emotions into maximum force), we could see clearly that it is **us**.

I am repeating myself for two reasons.

One, History repeats itself.

Two, science tells us that people need to hear things seven times before they GET IT. We only have one chance to get it. Will WE?

When I explained all of this to a friend, he clearly understood and said: "If we don't get it soon and do something different…we deserve this horrible ending of civilization."

Now I know my friend is intelligent and compassionate. He was just saying the truth off the top of his head. He was right. Why aren't we listening to Behavior Scientists and putting their thoughts first in the world? If we were making progress as humans, we would find ways to stop children around the world from dying, stop the killing of a thousand elephants a month, stop destroying the water and the air. Instead we watch the news.

We are smart enough to go to the moon and back, but we can't stand next to another human being because of our negative emotions. There is only one problem and one answer in the universe – our germ, negative emotions, and the solving of that lethal germ. Have you ever felt that the universe was laughing at you…and you were the last to know? Well, you need not live in darkness anymore!

Wake up people, before you can't.

The number one consciousness of man should be, and hopefully will be, who we are, our history, and where we are going. The answer is to stop thinking we are good, right, in control. The answer is for an individual, a genius, two geniuses, a group, behavioral scientists, a government, researchers of the brain and all people that KNOW and CARE to come forward, empowered and honestly say:

The most significant forces with in human beings and the cause of our terrible problems are: our hormones, DNA, electrical chemistry, the use of our brains in different areas that continue negative emotions.

The studies prove this and more studies will make it astonishingly clear: We hate from the inside out! It's not over there! The answer is inside us…..not them.

When people and science use the WEB, documentaries, books or speeches to put first what needs to be first, we will have done the right thing.

As long as we continue to be weak, cowardly and self-righteous; as long as we continue to say it's not our fault; as long as we continue to say we are good and in control of the earth and other human beings we will not be able to admit: NEGATIVE EMOTIONS RUN US AND THE WORLD. If we don't wake up and take responsibility for our animalness, it will result in the end of mankind, our ego, all consciousness and the God inside of us.

THE GIFT

We have talked a lot about hate, but there is one emotion that is bigger – FEAR.

The worst fear is fear of the unknown. Just like hate, fear of the unknown is in our DNA, our blood and our adversarial will.

Here is one last story.

The Gift is an episode from the television program The Twilight Zone and it aired on 4/27/62. The location, Modero, Mexico. Time frame, 1950's when the village is alarmed by a light from space. A strange man is found. He speaks differently from them. He is hurt from a crash landing of his spacecraft. The town's people put him in a room to try and heal. A young boy befriends the stranger and feels the goodness and warmth coming from the wounded alien.

The town gathers in their fear and shout:

"Look out for the boy!"

"He is attaching the boy!"

"He's killing the boy!"

They shoot the stranger, dead.

Turns out the stranger had some material in his hand. The Police Chief asks the Doctor what the note said and was read what remained:

"Greetings to the people of Earth. We come as friends and in peace. We bring you this gift. The following chemical formula is a vaccine against all forms of cancer..."

Unknown fear is right in front of us IN OUR HANDS.